IMPACT VIRTUALLY

HOW TO MAXIMIZE YOUR IMPACT ... WITHOUT GOING ANYWHERE

A practical guide to personal influence in an increasingly virtual and digital world.

First published in 2017 by

Clinton Wingrove,
Camberley, UK

Copyright © Clinton Wingrove, 2017

All rights reserved. No part of this work may be reproduced, transmitted, stored in a retrieval system, modified, or made publicly available, in any form or by any means without prior written permission of the publisher.

Book design & layout by Velin@Perseus-Design.com

ISBN:
978-1-9997081-0-8 (Paperback)
978-1-9997081-1-5 (e-book)

Disclaimer
All the information, techniques, skills and concepts contained within this publication are of the nature of general comment only and are not in any way recommended as individual advice.

Should any reader choose to make use of the information contained herein, this is their decision, and the author and publisher does not assume any responsibilities whatsoever under any conditions or circumstances.

Printed in the United Kingdom

To all those who have ideas and talent to share, and who are inhibited by this noisy, virtual, and largely digital world.

All the time that world still has challenges, it awaits your contributions and impact; go ahead and make them.

CONTENTS

Introduction vii
Chapter 1 THE MYTHS OF IMPACTING VIRTUALLY 1
Chapter 2 FOCUSING YOUR MESSAGE 11
Chapter 3 YOUR VIRTUAL BRAND MATTERS 19
Chapter 4 MANAGING YOUR PRESENCE 33
Chapter 5 MAKING SPECIFIC IMPACTS 43
Chapter 6 USING CONTEMPORARY TECHNOLOGY 59
Chapter 7 MAKING "LUMPY" VIRTUAL IMPACT 67
Epilogue 71
Appendix 1 PERSONAL BRAND WORKSHEET 73
Appendix 2 DISRESPECTFUL BEHAVIORS 77
Impact Virtually Products & Services 81

INTRODUCTION

First, let me tell you what this book is **not**.

This is **not** another book about selling on the internet using social media. This is also **not** another book about how to speak or make presentations. While those are related topics, the focus here is on **you**; it provides techniques to enable you to achieve **Impact Virtually**.

This book is about how you can impact others in an increasingly noisy, virtual, and largely digital world – how to enhance **your** personal effectiveness; how to get more of **your** ideas heard and adopted; how to improve **your** relationships; … without necessarily going anywhere!

Why do you need it? Because, how people interact with each other continues to change fundamentally. This demands that **you** change how **you** connect with and influence others – to make **your** impact.

> I recall with much amusement the day that my son brought his new girlfriend home to have dinner with us. My wife greeted them warmly but advised that "Once we have eaten, there is a program on TV that I want to watch. I'd like peace and quiet; after that, we can chat as much as you like."

After dinner, silence obediently ensued. But the end of the program was signposted by a shrill, "I've been watching you! You've been texting each other!" from my wife. Sure enough, my son and his girlfriend had been sitting on the sofa, texting each other.

My son's response was classic. "No mother. We have been communicating ... while you have merely been staring at a plastic box."

Yes, communication is now handled through many media in a virtual world. And so, how we impact each other has also changed.

- For many of us, face-to-face communications now play a minor role in our interactions. But, face-to-face can still be highly effective. You should not give up on it lightly just because virtual and digital means are quicker or easier.

- Your boss, your parents, and those in authority no longer have control over what you say, when or to whom. But, you must be even more careful what you say, how and to whom.

- Through technology, many of your "conversations" now take place across time, space, languages, and cultures.

- Things you have "said" get forwarded and re-circulated. You often do not even know who received them. But, they **all** accumulate and make an impact ... **your** impact.

- The virtual world is busy, noisy and distracting. So, messages need to be clear, targeted, and often repeated, repeated, repeated, ... if they are to be heard.

Introduction

- People expect rapid responses, extended periods during which you are responsive, and they have shortening attention spans. The timing and length of your messages are therefore critically important.

Think about the last time you interacted with someone who was not physically with you - perhaps by phone, by video conference, via social media, using collaborative tools, by email or text, or even via the written word. These are all virtual communications.

- Did you think beforehand about the impact you wanted to achieve? Or, were you mainly reactive?

- Did you achieve the impact you hoped for? Do you even know?

- Do you know the **cumulative** effect of all your interactions with that person? Are they net-positive or net-negative?

- Did you unintentionally impact others at the same time? Do you know and, if so, whom? Was there collateral impact?

- Did you reflect on what happened to learn how you could do better next time? Or, do you always communicate in the same way?

How we now communicate with and impact each other is analogous to brain activity. Thousands of bite-sized communications or **connectives**™ combine to create or destroy, reinforce or diminish, sustain or erase, use or abuse our relationships. And, our relationships are what we use to achieve impact.

™ Connective and Connectives are Trade Marks of Clinton Wingrove, 2017

We now live in a different world fueled by such **connectives**. Let me define **connectives** and a few other words that I'll use throughout this book:

- CONNECTIVES

    Connectives (Noun) Brief, transient connections between people, processes, and things; across space, time, languages, and cultures.

    i.e., The many interactions that now take place, largely supported by technology, and that make up most of our communications and create our impact.

    They each may take the form of a sentence exchanged at a water-cooler, a tweet, an email, a comment during a teleconference, a facial expression made during a videoconference, a note posted in a collaboration tool, or a reaction when someone else enters the room.

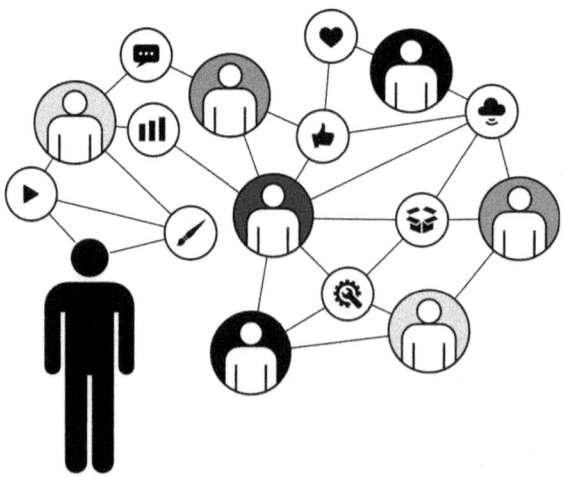

Introduction

Collections of virtual **connectives** have largely replaced lengthy face-to-face discussions, letters and memos of old.

The person-to-things and person-to-processes **connectives** are relatively new but rapidly expanding in number as we make greater use of voice-activated gadgets, sensors, and artificially intelligent devices, and of SaaS process-support technology.

Your relationships with others, and thus **your** potential to impact and influence them, are built from these many **connectives**.

- IMPACT

    Any effect that you seek to have on someone else. This can include, e.g.,

    - You seek a promotion and want to influence a range of people to enable you to get the job.

    - You want to establish yourself as the expert in a certain field so that you are asked to speak at conferences.

    - You frequently attend meetings and are frustrated because you never seem to be able to get yourself heard.

    - You have an idea for a new way of working in your team and want to get them to support you.

    - You and your partner are currently living miles apart, and you want to win their heart.

Think about this question, "What do you want them to think, feel, believe, say, or do?" You must make the impact needed to achieve that.

- **VIRTUALLY**

  By any means other than physically face-to-face with the other person(s). This might be synchronous (e.g., by telephone or video conference) or asynchronous (e.g., by email, social media, collaboration tools, …).

- **SOCIAL MEDIA**

  Any technology that supports blogs, posts, tweets, … and responses to them between groups of users.

Keep it EASY!

Despite decades of attempts to "Keep It Simple, Stupid" (KISS), things continue to get more complex. But the real challenge is **not** to make things simple – rather, to make them **easy**. And, achieving impact **is** easy – you just have to know how, and to discipline yourself to do it.

> "I remember a remark of Albert Einstein, which certainly applies to music. He said, in effect, that everything should be as simple as it can be, but not simpler," Roger Sessions.

To achieve impact in a virtual environment, you need many of the same skills you need in the face-to-face world. But, you need them in different proportions, **and** you need a few additional skillsets.

Introduction

These are the four broad skill or activity sets you need to Impact Virtually:

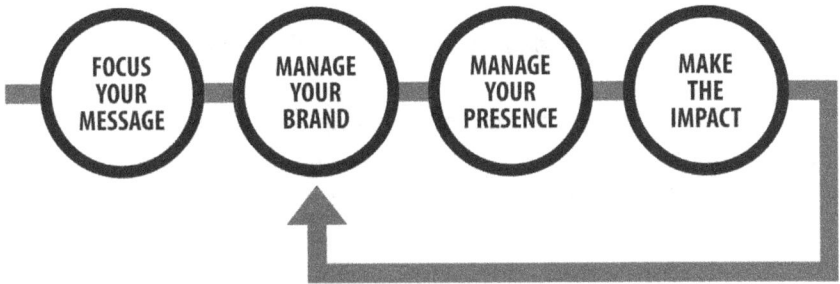

- Focus your MESSAGE

    Always know the messages that you need to communicate, and to whom you need to communicate them to achieve your desired impact.

- Manage your BRAND

    Make sure that you are known for what you want and need to be known for.

- Manage your PRESENCE

    Make sure that you are present, i.e., "seen" and "heard" by the right people, at the right time, using the right medium.

    And, make sure that you are mentally present when you are seeking to make an impact, i.e., attentive to what is being said and what is happening around you.

- Make a specific IMPACT

    To make a specific impact, you need to manage the 6 C's:

    1. Contact – Identify and contact those you need to impact.

    2. Connect – It is the relationship that matters.

    3. Curiosity – Ensure they want to and will hear you.

    4. Conviction – Deliver powerfully and persuasively.

    5. Commitment – Get commitment to act.

    6. Closure – Ensure impact achieved.

This book will equip you to master those skillsets!

We will conclude with some thoughts on:

   How best to engage with contemporary technology.

   Making "lumpy"[1] virtual impact.

---

[1] "Lumpy" is used to describe physical items such as brochures, post-cards, give-aways, letters, …

Chapter 1
THE MYTHS OF IMPACTING VIRTUALLY

We all know that technology is advancing at a continuously increasing rate and that it should solve all our problems. We are bombarded with advice on how to use it. So, how come impacting others seems ever more difficult?

Put simply, technology is not the panacea solution. Nor is all the advice necessarily relevant to you.

There are many myths, including but not limited to:

Myth 1 - Size Matters!

… or your capacity to create impact is measured by the size of your contact list.

In some cases, that may be true. But building a huge list of "contacts" who don't really know you and whom you don't need to impact is clearly of little value.

> *Recently, I attended a workshop on using Social Media for sales. Each attendee was asked to share the number of contacts they had on a specific social media site. Ensuing discussions addressed the benefits that were being experienced. These clearly revealed that those with shorter lists were gaining more benefits from the service – they typically had much stronger relationships with their contacts and could leverage them more effectively.*

Connecting with, and building relationships with, the people who really matter to you is critically important.

So, focus your first efforts on identifying the people you need to impact and connecting **well** with those … and, avoid connecting with those who merely seek to sell you something or simply found you on the internet.

Recommendations:

Focus more on building strong connections and relationships than on growing the size of your contact list.

> **Do not agree to connect with people who randomly invite you; they probably only want to sell you something.**

Myth 2 - Social Media Is King!

… or social media is now the way to achieve influence virtually.

Yes, it is **a** way. But, if you really want to make an impact, you need to do more than tweet, post, and blog. Those may merely create noise.

> *I was speaking recently with an inspirational speaker. He invested heavily in web-presence and social media marketing. However, he was staggered to discover that a campaign he conducted using hard-copy mail to his prospects had secured a 400% better response rate than his electronic marketing.*

Similarly, Likes, Comments, and Shares do not always equate to an increased influence. But, they do increase your **presence** – and that is a key part of the Impact Virtually puzzle.

Recommendation:

> Don't sign-up for Social Media tools just because others do.
>
> Don't seek to connect with everyone that social media sites suggest to you. Select only those you know could be valuable.

Myth 3 - There Is A Magic Digital Tool That Can Do It All!

Yeah … right! Even if that were true today, it won't be the same tomorrow, as technology is constantly evolving. There are analysts who now devote their time merely to reviewing new social media tools and recommending those we should now use, e.g., "The 39 I use every day," and "The top 50 social media sites."

Unless a key part of your brand is being an early adopter - up with the trends, the one who knows the cool stuff - it is best to make excellent use of a few tools rather than wasting time trying to keep up-to-date, dipping into many, or hopping from one to another.

Regularly review what is working amongst the type of people you need to impact, e.g.,

- The way recruiters find out about applicants is continuously changing. Sending a resume used to work. Now a profile on a professional networking site can be critically important – and, inappropriate content on a social site can be damaging.

- If you want to be known as an expert in your field, then posting content on professional discussion forums or even your own blog-site can be valuable.

- If you want an internal promotion, then making active, positive use of internal collaboration tools, and of communication tools such as email and document sharing can be valuable.

Recommendations:

Make robust, evidence-based choices with a long-term focus.

Ask your peers what they use and for what. Ask what benefits they experience.

Evaluate each digital tool's relevance to your goals. Check if the benefits outweigh the effort and cost involved.

Myth 4 - You Should Post New Content Every Day

Are you really so important that people will want to read your material every day **and** will be impressed by it?

If you flood people with information, they may just create a rule that sends all your communications to the trashcan!

> *Dr. Martin Hilbert and his team at the University of Southern California used a complex formula to calculate the average amount of information stored – and sent – in the world – from every medium from computers to paper and books – to letters in the post[2]. Using the analogy of an 85-page newspaper, they found that in 1986 we received around 40 newspapers full of information every day, but this had rocketed to 174 in 2007. And, it continues to rise. So much data that most are forgotten almost instantly.*

Review whether your impact truly is dependent on material that you proactively share ... then, decide how often and where to share it.

Recommendations:

> Ask yourself whether posting material on-line is really going to boost your personal brand and help you to make an impact on your target audience. Is the cost of your time outweighed by the potential benefit?

---

[2] "Welcome to the information age – 174 newspapers a day ..." <http://www.telegraph.co.uk/news/science/science-news/8316534/Welcome-to-the-info>.

Myth 5 - Make Yourself Stand Out

In a virtual world, and if you want to make an impact, you need to find ways to make yourself memorable ... but **for the right reasons**. Including animals in videos has been shown to increase the number of views and their impact considerably. But, would having a parrot on your shoulder add positively to **your** brand?

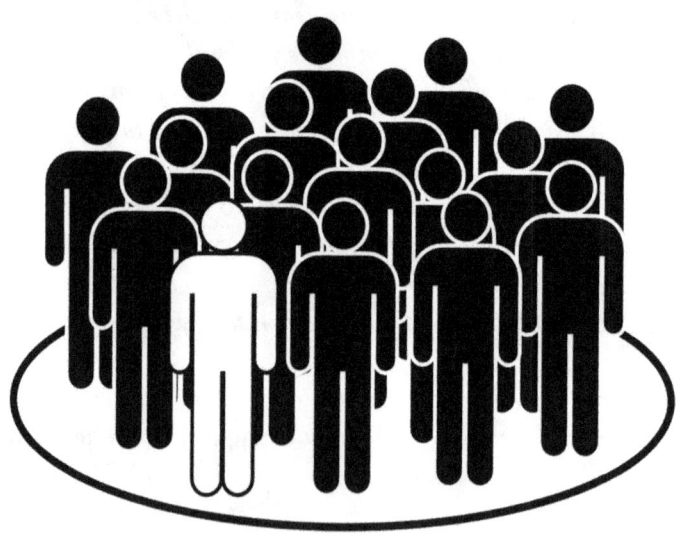

To make an impact, you need to make your views and ideas stand out in the right way.

> *An example is the "Lean in 15" author, Joe Wicks. He gives similar advice to many other health coaches, but he used quirky 15-second social media posts to make himself a personality and make the advice easily digestible for the user. He's gone from being a personal trainer earning £25,000/ year to a triple best-selling author.*

But, his approach might not have been appropriate if he had wanted to be the world's best funeral director.

However, taking a unique stance on something comes with its own risks. You may be perceived negatively, e.g., opinionated, disruptive, etc. even if your intent is positive. So, take care!

Recommendations:

> *Make sure your uniqueness is known.*
>
> *Make sure your message stands out and ensure that everything you do and say adds value to your brand, and represents you how you want and need to be viewed.*
>
> *Be authentic!*

Myth 6 - Keep It Simple, Stupid!

Wow. Hasn't this KISS message taken hold! But, short, simple messages often run the risk of being misunderstood. Here's a commonly used example:

"I never said she stole the money."

I am reliably informed that this can have over 20 **significantly different** meanings with all the consequent potential ramifications, e.g.,

- If you emphasize only the first word "I," the implication is that **someone else** said she stole the money.

- If you emphasize only the last word, the implication is that it was something **other than money** that may have been stolen.

When communicating virtually, it is not always easy to achieve the desired emphasis or to confirm the other party's understanding. That is obviously true whether using emails, tweets, posts, blogs, comments, or memos. But, it can also be true during teleconferences and video conferences.

If you want to make an impact, you must take responsibility for what others understand, not merely for what you say.

Recommendation:

> *Some messages are complex and can get lost in translation and simplification. Focus on the clarity of your message, not merely on conciseness and simplicity.*

Myth 7 - Everything Should Be Visual

Advances in the sophistication and accessibility of tools for creating visual images have led to an explosion in the use of graphics.

Yes, visuals create a powerful psychological impact; "A picture can say more than a thousand words."

But, the same tools can also mislead or confuse with the same power! So, take care when using them. Make sure that your visuals definitely will be interpreted appropriately.

> *"Believe only half of what you see and nothing that you hear,"*
> Edgar Allan Poe,

However, there is a very powerful form of visual communication that we risk losing as we live more in our virtual world – body language, including facial expressions.

There is already technology that reads body language and facial expressions, and produces an analysis of it. But, widespread use of it is not yet here. When it becomes generally available, we will all become even more conscious of how we look!

In the meantime, making use of video for virtual communications can enable you to pick up those clues about:

- the other party's understanding of your messages

- what they are thinking or concluding, and

- how they are feeling.

Recommendation:

> Don't use visuals for the sake of it. Ensure that they add to your impact by clarifying the message, reinforcing its importance, and aiding others to remember it.

Myth 8 - Popularity Equals Impact.

Likes and shares do not always equate to impact. They can give a good indication of reaction, but not subsequent action.

Recommendation:

> *Measure your success by the positive actions that have come out of your influencing activity, not by the volume of superficial responses.*

Those are just eight of the more common myths about what you need to do to make an Impact Virtually.

Let's move on to explore what **does** work, and how **you can use it** to increase your personal impact and influence in a variety of circumstances.

Chapter 2

FOCUSING YOUR MESSAGE

Ever spent time talking with someone and only later realized that you could have used that time with them to far greater effect?

Ever spent time trying to persuade someone to commit to something only to find out later that it was someone else who had the final say?

Ever been on a teleconference or video conference and come away frustrated because those you needed to influence were not engaged?

Ever been to a networking meeting and come away having only spoken with people you already knew or with whom you share no interests?

What's the issue?

The above are four examples of thousands of interactions that happen every day because people have not focused their message (content), and/or not focused on their target audience.

Why does it matter?

- If you don't define the **specific messages** that you need to get across to people, you miss opportunities to do so; limit your impact; and risk sending an incorrect message.

- If you don't define the **type** of people you need to impact, you cannot structure your arguments, select the best medium, or even locate them to connect with.

- If you don't identify the specific **individuals** you need to influence, you cannot locate and connect with them, or learn about their wants and needs, etc.

What can you do?

1. Focus your messages

You must be clear about the messages that you need to get across - the things that you need people to **think, feel, believe, say, or do** as a result of your impact.

So, start by thinking through and defining what those messages are.

2. Define the <u>type</u> of people you need to impact.

In some cases, it will be clear at the outset whom you need to influence and the environment in which you will get the best opportunity to do so. In other cases, you may need to think hard about who your targets really are.

e.g., If you want a promotion, your target types could include:

- Managers of the role(s) that you would like
- HR staff who recruit into those roles
- Individuals who are exceptional in those roles
- Managers who are served by those roles
- Individuals who can give you an introduction.

e.g., If you want to get a budget approved, your target types could include:

- Your immediate manager
- Peers who will be competing for the same pot of money
- The management accountant for your area
- The people whom you will serve if you get the budget approved

and, of course,

- The budget holder and those who have their ear! (their secretary or PA is always a great person to make an impact on. They are the gatekeeper to your main target after all!)

e.g., If you want to get a specific action agreed to during an upcoming teleconference, your target types could include:

- The meeting chair
- Your immediate manager
- Those who will be attending the teleconference
- Those who will not be attending the teleconference
- Those who will be affected by the outcome.

e.g., If you want to become known as the expert in a particular field, your target types could include:

- Other professionals working in that field
- Academics doing research in that field
- Executives in businesses who use that expertise
- Writers, bloggers, etc. who write on that topic.

3. Identify the specific individuals you need to influence

There will be occasions when you need to influence many people, and occasions when you need to influence only one or a few. So, the better you can define, identify and then target individuals, the greater chance you have of achieving impact.

From your list of the **types** of people you need to impact, you then need to find out **who** they are. Of course, you may already know many of them. To find out the others, social media and other technology tools can play a useful role, enabling you to search for and learn about individuals.

Depending on the types of people you are seeking to identify, you could:

- Use your own contact list

- Ask existing contacts if they know them

- Use networking groups – searching, asking others, posting a discussion topic, going to their meetings, …

- Use discussion forums – searching, posting a discussion topic, …

- Use blogs – searching, posting a discussion topic, …

- Make internet and intranet searches

- Refer to organization charts

- Look up membership lists and lists of officers of groups, organizations, …

- Go back to lists of attendees at prior meetings

- Read newsletters, newspapers, ….

NOTE: At this point, you are not necessarily making real **connections**, merely establishing a potential **contact** list.

Now, you need to know about each of these potential contacts, e.g.,

- Do you know someone who can introduce you to them?

- Do you have a shared interest with them that you can use as a reason to establish contact?

- Do they belong to any social media groups with you?

- Do you have their contact details such as email, telephone number, address, …?

- What is their background?

- What relationship, if any, do they already have with you?

- What are their opinions/positions on the issue(s) relating to how we might wish to influence or impact them?

- What are **their** brands?

Chapter 3
YOUR VIRTUAL BRAND MATTERS

When you attempt to influence someone else, their view of your brand is their starting point; it is the context into which they slot everything that you say and do.

What is the issue?

- FACT: You already have a virtual brand – even if you don't know what it is?

    You have a virtual brand even if you have never accessed a social media site, sent a text, or taken a "selfie." You may be noted as much for your absence as by your presence.

    Even Neanderthals had individual brands; some were known as the tough fighters; some as the hunters; and some as those who took care of others... and that affected their life-chances. As does your brand today!

- FACT: Everything you do and say affects your brand

    Every post, every comment, every text, every tweet, every comment you make at the water-cooler, every photo, every email, and even that laugh on the recent videoconference ... they **all** aggregate into **your brand**.

    Even what you do not do and what you do **not** say can have a cumulative effect.

Why does it matter?

- How other people view you is critically important.

    It impacts how others engage with you, and even whether they engage with you at all.

    It is the filter through which others process all your communications, e.g.,

    If you have a positive brand, mistakes are viewed as minor aberrations.

    If you have a negative brand, mistakes are viewed as "Typical!"

    Your brand informs and may even determine the decisions others make about you. Your brand influences greatly what others share amongst themselves about you ... and that further defines your brand.

IT AFFECTS YOUR ENTIRE LIFE!

- Your brand evolves. If you do not manage it, others do that for you!

- Your brand may be different in various situations.

Many years ago, I worked with someone who was a highly professional PA, with a very quiet and reserved demeanor. Imagine my astonishment when I discovered that a few times a week, she and her partner traveled hundreds of miles to compete at very high-level Latin-American dancing competitions!

Today, the above scenario would be highly unlikely as videos of my colleague dancing would be in the public domain before she had left the competition!

What can you do?

If you seek to make an impact virtually, and to manage that impact, you must:

- Know your brand

    Know what you want it to be and what is currently is.

    And, **keep up-to-date** with how you are perceived - it can change in a flash.

- Build your brand

    You must be proactive in building your brand and ensuring that it is seen as consistent, especially by all those you wish to impact.

- Protect your band.

    Others may try to damage your brand. Some may do so inadvertently. You may even damage your own brand by accident.

    You must be vigilant, monitor your brand, and take steps to protect it.

1. Know your brand

First, you must decide what brand you want. Knowing the brand you already have is a good place to start. So, let's look at that first.

Recommendation:

> *There is a worksheet in Appendix 1 that you can use to clarify your brand. You may wish to review this before reading on.*
>
> *You can download a Word document version from:*
> http://clintonwingrove.com/IVfreestuff

Here are some steps you can take to assess your current brand:

- Do an internet search of your full name (with quotation marks around it, e.g., "Clinton Wingrove"). Do you appear in the results? If not, should you? If you do, read what appears as though you are reading it about someone else. Do you like what you see?

- Access the social media sites that you normally use. Look at your public profile as though it is about someone else and you are viewing it for the first time. Does this present you in the way that will enhance your impact with your target audience?

- Access the social media sites that you know the people you want to impact use. Search to see if you appear and, if so, how. Examine what comes up about the people you hold in high regard – how does it compare to what comes up about you?

- Take part in a 360 Degree Feedback process, asking for responses from people whose opinions you value, and from those whom you would like to influence.

- Identify a small number of people, e.g., your manager, colleagues, friends, and family members. Ask them how they believe you may be perceived[3].

- Identify some events, meetings, gatherings, … to which you believe you should have been invited. Were you?

- Identify some discussions that have taken place in which you believe you should have played a key role. Were you invited to do so?

2. Build your brand

The more you are in control of your brand, the better use you can make of it.

Do you want to be known as:

- The leader - inspirational and forward thinking?

- The manager - taking action to get things done?

- Someone with commercial acumen, always spotting the opportunities for deals and growing the business?

---

[3] The wording here is very deliberate. Do not ask, "How do you perceive me?" That may be too challenging for some people, and they might not tell you the truth. Instead, ask, "How do you believe I am perceived by others." The latter allows them to distance themselves from any critical comments which they feel you should hear.

- Someone who is personally effective?
- …?

You must decide.

Having decided, you need to take consistent steps to build and sustain that brand. The key word is **consistency**. Your brand is built from what you do and say consistently.

Recommendation:

> *You may wish to go back to the worksheet and annotate it with the changes you would like and/or need to make.*

You can use all manner of tools to manage your virtual brand:

- Face-to-face meetings

    Impacting virtually is not only about using virtual tools. Sometimes, the occasional face-to-face connection can work wonders … so long as that face-to-face meeting is with the right person(s) and it is effective.

- Phone calls – speaking to individuals is still OK! In fact, rarity is making it even more impactful.

    Make a note of the people with whom you need to build a stronger relationship and schedule times in the future to call them and catch-up.

- Teleconferences and video conferences.

Identify appropriate upcoming opportunities to seize airtime. Then, grab them.

- Social media – connecting and posting comments, discussion topics, blogs, articles, ... that add to your credibility.

  Maintain your profile and make it as consistent across sites as possible, always reinforcing your desired brand.

  Post comments and discussions that demonstrate your beliefs, values, and expertise, and your stance on matters that are important to you.

  Give credit to and build on comments that come from those you seek to impact – they will likely reciprocate.

- Email – use well and sparingly.

  Send **individual** emails to those with whom you need to develop stronger relationships, perhaps providing further information than in more widely circulated copy.

  Avoid using long copy lists and REPLY TO ALL as much as possible. It annoys people!

  You don't need to use such openings as "Dear Clinton," but using an individual's name in your opening does make it feel more personal.

  Use appropriate salutations to close such as "Very best regards," or "Yours sincerely." They really do still help and almost never have a negative impact.

- Text messages.

   Take care with emoticons. Some people simply don't understand them, and some don't view them as cute or funny – rather, as childish - know your audience!

   Take care with chat abbreviations or **textese** (also known as **txt-speak, txtese, chatspeak, txt, txtspk, txtk, txto, texting language, txt lingo, SMSish, txtslang, txt talk**[4] ... note the opportunity for confusion!). Many people still consider those who use them to be **BAM** (Below Average Mentality).

- Your own website – this can be your personal showcase and billboard.

   Ensure that your employer, if any, is happy with you doing so as this may be a conflict of interest.

- Networking meetings – this may seem odd in a book on "virtual" impact, but networking meetings can have a very significant impact virtually.

   One of their most valuable contributions is, if used well, they send a number of people away knowing you and what you do – hopefully, to share that information with others, thereby adding to your virtual brand.

- How you speak

---

[4] "SMS language - Wikipedia." <https://en.wikipedia.org/wiki/SMS_language>.

You don't need to attend elocution classes or to change your accent deliberately. However, how you speak is one of the major factors affecting your ability to impact others.

Pay attention to your target audience; listen to their use of language, the words, phrases, acronyms, etc. that they use.

However, do learn to speak and present with impact.

- How you dress (whether we like it or not, with increasing use of video, it has an effect).

I don't hanker for the days of suit, shirt, and tie. But, if you want to finesse your impact, learning about the expectations of your target audience, and dressing appropriately can make a positive difference.

Appearing in a onesie will certainly make an impact, but will it be the one you want?

- How you behave

You may be the smartest person in your field and have the "gift of the gab," but that is no guarantee that you will have the impact you seek.

Many years ago, I was seeking an expert in complex problem-solving techniques to work with some technical teams. I found such an individual and invited him to meet with me. He duly arrived, a little early, and demanded to be allowed to make his own way to my office – something our internal security procedures prohibited. On being advised of this, he ranted at the receptionist *and left! To this day, I know that he is still the best in his field ... but **I will never work with him nor refer him**.*

Extreme case? Yes. But, disrespectful behavior abounds and virtual communications seem to encourage, or at least, propagate it. Think carefully about the image that you present – are you viewed as someone deserving respect?

A list of common disrespectful behaviors is shown in Appendix 2.

3. Protect your brand

Companies don't only build their brands; they also passionately protect them. They do that because it matters. You also need to protect your brand.

- Think twice before posting anything on the internet, especially if you think it's funny – retrospectively, it often isn't!

    Do you really want to be remembered as the guy with the stupid hat, doing handstands in the car park?

    Do you really want to be known for looking sultry with big, red, pouting lips?

    Does that ironic tweet or tongue-in-cheek comment have the potential to be misinterpreted horribly?

- Set your email system so that your emails don't go immediately when you click "SEND." Make sure that you must click "SEND ALL" or something similar. This gives you chance to reread what you have written and catch those "Oh, so easy to make" howlers!

- Be wary of "FORWARD", "REPLY ALL" or adding someone to a copy list on an email response. Make sure you read any included prior email chain (or delete it) so that any inappropriate earlier messages don't end up in the wrong hands and reflect badly on you.

- Actively track what is being said about you and respond **appropriately**.

- **Don't feed the trolls**. Nobody wins in a troll-fight and trolls know that but don't care – by posting negative comments or baiting you, they merely seek to bring you down to their level. So, don't take the bait!

However, ignoring some things may inadvertently sanction them.

Develop your own way of taking the moral high ground. An example response to a rude or destructive comment might be, "Thank you for commenting, Chris. You will appreciate that I respectfully disagree. If we can raise the tone of the debate, I'll be happy to re-engage and continue the discussion."

Personally, I actively comment on constructive posts, praise those who disagree with me in a respectful manner, and **ignore** any nonsense!

- View every teleconference, video conference, meeting, discussion forum, collaboration session, file sharing, email chain, social media exchange, text, ... as an opportunity to build your brand **and** for your brand to be undermined. Keep your brand front of mind and be cognizant of exchanges that could damage it.

Chapter 4

MANAGING YOUR PRESENCE

You cannot make an impact without being present. But, in the context of making a virtual impact, what does **present** mean?

First, you need to make sure that **you are physically present**. In the context of making an impact virtually, that can include: being on the teleconference or webinar, handling the email exchange, participating in the collaboration exercise, actively following the discussion group, ….

Second, you need to make **your presence felt**. Just being there is not enough.

Third, you need to be **mentally present**, i.e., attentive at the right time.

What is the issue?

- Just because you are on someone's contact list does not mean that you have a **connection**. If you are to achieve impact, the other person(s) needs to **feel** your presence. You need to establish a two-way connection or relationship. Just sending a connection request, an email, a text or leaving a voicemail is no assurance that you have a communication path.

    As I said to someone only a short while ago: Last year, I met the Prime Minister of a Caribbean island and now have his contact details and he has mine. But that is not much use. What would be so much more useful is if he was saying to someone else right now, "I met Clinton Wingrove and he [does] … I have his contact details if you want them. I recommend that you get in touch with him."

- Have you ever attended a meeting and been ignored throughout?

    That's because, for the others, you were not making your presence felt … or, perhaps, **they** weren't really present and paying attention!

- Have you ever attended a meeting hoping to influence a decision only to find that it seemed to have been wrapped up before you even got there?

    That's because someone prepared better than you did – they managed to be **present** and make an impact before the meeting!

Why does it matter?

- Think of the people whose opinions you hold dear.

    Trust and credibility, and thus the potential to impact, are usually established over a period of time and multiple interactions. You need to plan many of them.

- Think of how fleeting some of your contacts are – mere **"connectives"** - a few minutes on a telephone call; a brief text; a short email; a few minutes of agenda time on a tele or video conference; a Twitter message.

    Unless you master the art of establishing your **presence** in those few seconds, your impact will be limited or negative.

    Prepare! As the old saying goes,

    "By failing to prepare, you are preparing to fail,"
    Benjamin Franklin.

What can you do?

In 'the good old days', it was said that "It's not what you know, it's who you know."

Then the information revolution hit us and it became, "It's not who you know, it's what you know."

Well, in this virtual and largely digital world, it is swinging towards "It's not who you know or what you know, **It's who knows you**."

> *If we search for a plumber, we refer to web-sites looking for referrals; if we find a potential new employee, we seek references; we review star ratings on shopping sites; professional service firms say that despite all their mass advertising, most of their new business comes from referrals; ….*

We all do this because we trust making decisions based on others' **reputations** and referrals.

Guess what? That's how you are judged… by your reputation and brand!

The simple fact is that you must be **known by the right people for the right reasons at the right time**.

> *Many years ago, I worked with an organization which, with hindsight, had one of the most effective processes for finding internal candidates to fill vacancies.*
>
> *As soon as the vacancy appeared, the hiring manager would inform one of his team about it, someone who understood their role.*

He would then wait approximately a week and call them back in. He asked two questions, "So, who do they think will get the position and why?"

Following some quick checks of the individual identified, if he found nothing untoward, he offered that person the job - with frequent high success rates.

His logic? The process elicited a wide range of informed input from people he could probably never have had truly open discussions with about such a sensitive issue. Few people would be surprised by the decision, making it easier to implement. And, it was extremely efficient ... for him.

Who got identified? Those who were most well-known. Well – for positive things. Well – by more people in the process.

You need to ensure that you are known by the right people, for the right things, at the right time, e.g.,

- If you are seeking to get a decision on budgets in an upcoming teleconference, you need to be known by the key decision makers in that meeting as someone who has their finger on the finances ... don't wait until the meeting and depend solely on logic, and your negotiating skills.

- If you are seeking to get a promotion, you need to be known by the key decision makers as someone who fits the profile, who passionately seeks the role, and who can be trusted to add value once in it ... don't wait until the interview.

- If you are seeking to influence a choice of suppliers, you need to be known by the decision maker(s) as someone who has done their homework, has expertise in the area, and will actively support the right decision ... don't wait until the first discussion or someone else has put forward their preference.

Being **present** virtually is not only about being on the teleconference, the video conference, the email circulation list, ... It is also about being **uppermost in the minds** of those you seek to influence.

Managing your **presence** is about ensuring that when you make any direct input, those to whom it is directed are already **attentive and curious** to know what **you** have to add.

They will then be influenced more easily and more effectively.

Managing your presence is, therefore, about:

- Knowing at all times when and where you need to be known, by whom and for what

- Skillfully targeting your brand

- Building your credibility

- Managing your relationships **before** you need them

- Establishing trust with your connections

- Earning their respect.

Here are some ideas for you to consider:

- Identify an upcoming virtual meeting and the impact you need to achieve? Think about who you need to influence and in what way.

  What can you do virtually before the meeting to increase your chance of success by managing your presence?

  e.g., reach out to ask about their wants and needs; send them something helpful, even if not directly related to the upcoming meeting; ...

- Identify an upcoming meeting that has people attending with whom you typically do not meet. List the people who will be there (in person or virtually).

  For each person, note what you know about them and their views; how you would like to connect with them; what they could do for you; what you could do for them.

  Fill in the gaps using virtual tools such as social media, search engines, emails to others, ...

  Now, how can you become better known by each of them in advance of the meeting?

- Review your public virtual face – how does it set the scene for any impact you seek to make

  e.g., if you are going to have an interview, does it tell a compelling story of why your next entry on your resume should be this job? What can you do to improve it?

- Think of someone you seek to influence.

  What can your next three connections with them be to move that forward, i.e., to increase how well they know you?

  e.g., email, voice-call, text message, social media post, collaborative media contribution, ...

- Review your contact list and, for each one, identify how they might be able to help you to achieve impact yourself

  What do they know, who do they know, what do they do that you could emulate, ...?

  Identify how you can become better known by them to further your cause.

- Think about a situation in which you seek to be more influential.

  What do you know that would add value?

  Who do you know who might contribute?

  What do you have that might be needed?

  How best can you flag these up to those who matter and ensure that you get the credit?

- Think about any upcoming virtual meeting(s).

  Who will be attending?

What do you know about their locations, their languages, their cultures.

Take some time to do a little research so that you can appear culturally sensitive and informed on the day.

- Think about any upcoming virtual meeting(s).

Who will be chairing the meeting? What can you do now to help them, especially in relation to your opportunity to make an impact?

e.g., can you send them materials in advance; suggest tools to use in the meeting; advise on how to do something; share some information that will make their job easier; ...

- Think about any upcoming virtual meeting(s). **Test your equipment and software**. Make sure that you will be in a suitable space with no interruptions and, if a video meeting, with adequate lighting.

You cannot be present if nobody can see or hear you.

Chapter 5

MAKING SPECIFIC IMPACTS

Over time, your brand lays a foundation which makes it easier or more difficult for you to make specific impacts such as influencing a decision; getting a project approved; gaining support for an idea; obtaining funds for something; …. You need to use this foundation to maximum effect.

What is the issue?

- It is often said that some people have "the gift of the gab," implying that they can sell anything by what they say. While being articulate is a valuable influencing skill, it is as easy to say too much as it is to say too little.

- To be influenced, individuals typically need to be taken through a process (which may even need to be repeated multiple times) before the desired outcome is achieved.

- When you are working with people face-to-face you get instant feedback on what you are saying; not so through many virtual means.

- There are many more distractions in a virtual world. However, in the virtual world, you may have more **opportunities** to create an impact.

- Dealing with people face-to-face, you tend to engage the instant that you connect. In a virtual world, you can contact thousands of people and never really connect with a single one of them.

- In a virtual world, the people you are seeking to engage with and persuade are probably also the targets of many other people. You may be a mere tinkling sound in a cacophony of sound!

Why does it matter?

- When attempting to influence someone, solely having the correct answer rarely achieves a decision in your favor. Being correct merely gives you the right to argue your case. Most decisions are choices between competing correct options, and they often involve a significant emotional component.

- If you are to achieve more than a mere background impact, you need to **engage** with target others and **persuade** them of your specific message (your capability and potential; your knowledge and skill; your proposition; your idea; your demands; ….).

What can you do?

We have already looked at THREE foundation skills you need to use:

- **Focusing your message** - defining and identifying your target contacts

- **Managing your brand**

- **Managing your presence**

    Be seen and heard by the right people, at the right time, for the right things. This is about ensuring that you do have the contact(s) and setting up the right opportunity to actively engage them.

To achieve significant impact, you need to be able to change people's minds, i.e., to sell your idea, proposal, ... or even yourself. Knowing and following a structured process for influencing others can:

- Make achieving impact much more efficient.

- Increase the scale of your impact.

- Reduce the risk of failure.

You need to apply the 6 C's process:

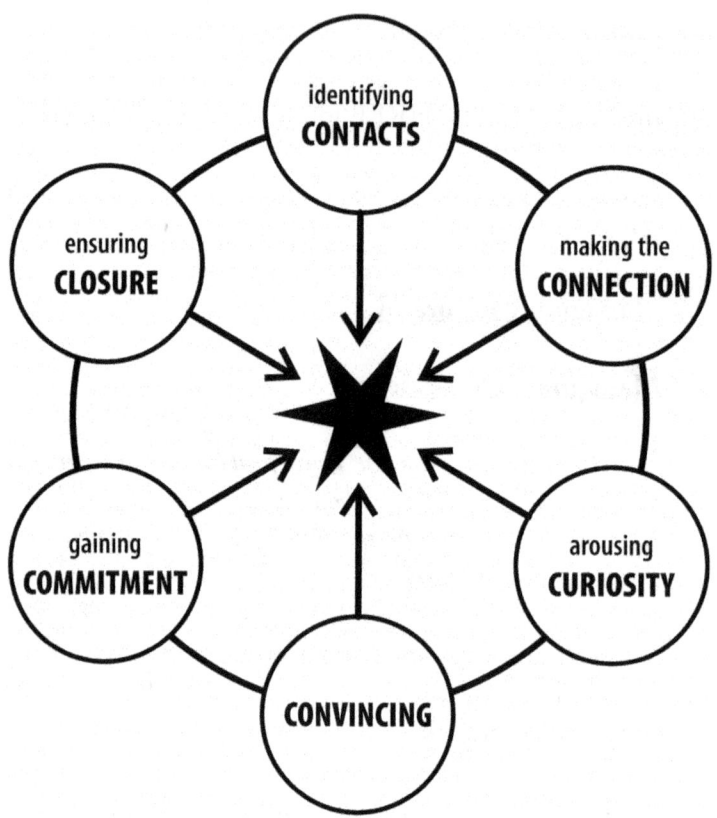

1. **Contact** – you must identify and contact all those whom you need to impact.

2. **Connect** – contact is not enough to achieve impact. You also need to **connect** with your targets, i.e., gain their attention so that they **can** hear your message. It is the **relationship** that matters more than the mere contact.

3. **Curiosity** – even if people **can** hear you (e.g., they receive your email, they are on the videoconference, they get your

text, …), that is no guarantee that they **want to** or **will** hear you (i.e., they **consciously** take notice).

Curiosity is about getting them interested enough in your message so that they want to hear more and so actively listen.

4. **Conviction** – once people are actively listening, you need to deliver your message concisely, powerfully, and persuasively. This requires planning, structure, and the use of influencing skills … and, you may need supportive evidence to back up your case.

5. **Commitment** – you must be sufficiently compelling to get them to commit to action.

6. **Closure** – you must ensure that your impact achieved your goal, i.e., they lived up to their commitment.

Each of these can be achieved via one or more interactions, which may include teleconferences, phone calls, email exchanges, file sharing, ….

As I said earlier, this is not a book about sales, but it is a book about how to sell yourself and your ideas in a virtual environment. So, what does that look like?

1. Making the Connection – Gaining Attention

Ever been in a video conference or even a meeting and noticed that other people were using their smartphones? Their attention had been lost – they were **disconnected**.

Ever been on a teleconference and suddenly you were asked a question but had no idea what had just been said? Your attention had been lost – you were **disconnected**.

Ever tried to have a conversation with someone you thought you "knew" but they seemed dismissive? They were probably **disconnected** from you.

You will never influence or persuade someone else of anything unless you make a real **connection**, i.e., gain and secure their attention. In our noisy virtual world, this is your first challenge.

For example:

- If you are working through email or text messages, think about how you will gain that attention if your email is one of a few hundred messages they receive each day.

    Think about your subject line or your first few words. Do they **grab** attention; do they connect directly with their hotspots, their key wants and needs, their passions, and beliefs?

- If you are working through collaborative tools, how are you going to make **your** edits and contributions standout without disrupting the work of others?

    Think about your use of fonts and colors; choose your timing so that your inputs are seen by others at their most receptive times.

- If you are on a teleconference or video conference, how are you going to gain airtime at the very point in the discussion when you need to make your points?

A technique used by professional interviewers to get control of a conversation is to use the other person's name – merely saying it will cause that person to pause long enough for you to step in.

Then, if more control is needed, ask them directly a closed question that they can answer easily. This creates another brief space to step into ... and closes out other attendees.

- If you are on a video conference, the above can be made even more effective by creating a sudden visual effect.

  e.g., putting your hands up nearer to the camera (which makes them look huge), suddenly changing the lighting, switching to a view of a slide or an object, ...

- If you are on social media, make a comment or post a discussion topic that you know will resonate with your targets; draw their attention to it specifically; ask for their responses; ...

How do you know if you have someone's attention?

Simple. When you communicate **to them**, you get a **prompt and related response** ... a virtual, "**I hear you**."

That "I hear you" may be verbal. It may also be visual, e.g., a smile or a shift of posture or direct eye contact.

2. Arousing Curiosity – Getting Them to Want to Hear More

Having someone's attention creates the possibility of influencing them. However, as the old saying goes,

> *"There are none as deaf as those who don't want to hear,"*
> *Anon*

Having attracted someone's attention and connected with them, you merely have them in a situation where they **can** hear you. You now must peak their curiosity so that **they want to hear** what you want to say. If not, you will quickly lose that attention. If you only have attention, you must push your messages at them. If they are curious, they are pulling information from you. The latter is therefore far more effective.

In a virtual environment, attention can be fleeting. It is common in video conferences to see other participants checking their email, reading texts, or even doing other quite unrelated activities. It's a bit like people who pick their noses while driving – they seem to think that you can't see them ... and probably don't care either!

To influence someone and create the impact that you seek, you need to ensure that your targets are listening - **listening because they want to hear what you might say**, i.e., they are Curious.

But, this effect will not be maximized if you give away too much too soon.

e.g., an email reads, "Clinton, I'd like a few minutes of your time tomorrow to explain why I believe that we should be reducing the budget on your Project X by $50,000. I'll share with you the costings and take you through how this will be more than enough to do what we need to do."

There are lots of reasons why I might not want to have that call!

Ensure that, as soon as you have the other party's attention, you make them curious about what you intend to say.

If you have completed the "Defining and Identifying your Targets" and "Managing Your Presence" steps well, you should have a good idea about what they want and need, etc. This will enable you to target your messaging.

e.g., if they have said that they want Project X to be a success for the whole team, you might say something like, "Clinton, I'd like a few minutes of your time tomorrow. I have been thinking about Project X and there's a way that we can secure real success for the team."

The principles behind this step are simple – arouse curiosity by promising something of interest or benefit that you can provide to the other party, keeping the details back ... tease them!

How do you know if you have aroused someone's Curiosity?

Simple.

When you communicate **to them**, you get a **prompt**, response like, "**Tell me more**." Ideally, this is going to be verbal. But, again, this may be visual like an encouraging smile or nod for you to continue.

3. Being Convincing – Presenting a Logical Case

To influence others, you must convince them about your position, i.e., you need to deliver a logical argument or case.

Your brand should give you a foundation of credibility.

You now need to call on your knowledge of, and evidence to support, your own case; your knowledge about them and their views; and your ability to handle any pushback that you may experience.

Don't hang around – curiosity wanes nearly as fast as attention, especially if it is not satisfied.

- Know what the critical points are, for whom and why.

- Communicate in a way that they will warm to – use the appropriate influencing currencies; appeal to their wants, needs, and interests; ….

- Present evidence to back up your claims, and explain the benefits and to whom they apply.

- Know what objections and questions may be presented, and be prepared to deliver your responses, preferably before you are called on to do so.

- Keep checking your progress, especially with those who are remote, by asking simple questions that do not emphasize the significance of what is being decided.

- If objections are raised or questions asked, test the relative importance of them before wasting time responding.

- When you have persuaded them, STOP - your work is done!

This is the critical step and one during which so many mistakes are made. Remember it is as easy to talk your way out of a commitment, as it is to achieve it in the first place.

Imagine the horror of the head of IT who had invested months researching the latest SaaS solutions for Performance and Talent Management.

He had shortlisted three suppliers, subjected them to a rigorous comparative pilot, and negotiated prices, support & maintenance, and terms & conditions. He had selected the best of the three and was now presenting this for final affirmation by the global leadership team. Nods and smiles all round.

As he was passing control of the video link for his slides over to the next speaker, he made the remark, "I'm glad we have gone with this option. It means that all our core HR processes are now managed by one vendor."

Immediately, the Finance Director from across the pond, who had been silent throughout, asked, "Doesn't that expose us to price increases if they know that we are totally dependent on them?"

Whether it did or not is not the issue. The point is that the comment was misplaced and the decision was put on hold pending further consideration and risk assessment.

****

An organization used to teach its technical center, having advised a client how to set-up their new purchase, to say, "Thank you for calling. If you get any problems, just call us. That is what we are here for."

That was until they realized that this was eliciting responses such as:

"Problems? What problems am I likely to experience?"

"Your real role is to handle problems! How many do you get then?"

There are many structures for managing this critical part of the process but the principles are all very similar:

- Ensure that your target is aware of the negative – the problem or pain that you are seeking to redress.

    Highlight this early. This is what they want to **get away from**.

    Without being conscious of this, why should they change?

- Make a claim(s) that you can fix the pain. This is what you need them to want to **go to**.

    This makes them curious.

- Present each key element of your proposal, idea, … - the most significant ones first – one at a time.

- Back up your claims and facts as needed with evidence, using a variety of credible sources, and calling on your brand.

- Answer potential objections and questions, preferably in advance of them being raised.

- Call upon any trustworthy support from within the target group to add credibility (call on your connections).

- Remind them of the pain and link each key element of your proposal, idea, ... to it to show its contribution to the solution.

- Check your progress so you can stop persuading at the earliest opportunity.

- At the earliest opportunity, seek clear and specific commitment if appropriate.

How do you know if you have convinced people?

Ask them and they will say something like, "**OK. I see your point**," or "**Yes, I get it,**" or "**That all makes sense**."

Sometimes, however, there will be a "but" on the end.

Be careful not to be side-tracked, many of these "buts" are merely deferring a decision.

Take steps to learn whether the other party would benefit irrespective of their "but." If so, they may just need an emotional push.

4. Gaining Commitment – Winning the Hearts

Have you ever seen something in a shop, decided to buy it but then left without doing so … only to get home and utter that well-known phrase, "I wish I had bought that …"?

The fact is that you were **convinced** about it (the logical argument around the need had won) but you did **not want it enough** at the time (the **emotional commitment** or **want** was not strong enough).

To be sure of achieving impact or the desired outcome, you may need to trigger the appropriate emotions to secure an overall commitment.

> *"People don't buy what you do, they buy why you do it,"*
> Simon Sinek

Having the correct answer is no guarantee of your ideas being accepted. To achieve real impact, you need to win the logical mind **and** win the heart.

You need to bring the future alive.

Through whatever medium you are using, transport the other party to a place and time when your ideas have already been accepted and implemented. Describe what it **is** like (yes, describe in the current tense).

> e.g., *"It's three years from now; we are in the senior leadership team meeting and reviewing the decision we made three years ago, to invest in System X.*
>
> *We are reflecting on all the old whining and moaning, the low engagement scores, the managers who would not do performance reviews.*

And, here we are now, savoring the freshly brewed coffee – 97% completion and still two weeks to go; staff morale is up; productivity is up; after a few well-deserved discipline cases, examples of poor performance have declined.

Jack stands up and we hear the fanfare he has set on his first slide – at last, we can see a list of the best managers ... and we can get them mentoring those who still need to develop their skills.

Isn't that what we are trying to achieve today?"

5. Ensuring Closure – Getting Action

Far too many great ideas remain as such ... merely ideas. If you really want to make an impact, you need to trigger action. So, you need to get closure on specific <u>actions</u> – what, by whom, and by when!

It is usually wise to get commitments in writing[5] as a closure step.

If securing the agreement is the critical component, then offer to document and circulate that. Specifically, get that on record as soon as possible using the medium at hand.

If the details of the agreement are critical, then

- Recap, involving all those who were parties to the "discussions."

---

[5] This is now usually taken to mean anything in hard copy and circulated electronic text (which typically adds a source, recipient, date and time).

- Ask the person who has committed to the agreement to send you their understanding.

Individuals feel far more committed to things that they have written down, especially if they are asked to send it in their own name or sign it. This also enables you to check early if there is any misunderstanding.

IMPORTANT: You have only achieved true impact if the things that you have argued for or promoted get implemented.

Don't leave that final and critically important step to others – **you** do the follow-up. Follow-up also gives you the opportunity to:

- Establish new connections

- Strengthen relations with those involved

- Identify other opportunities to achieve impact

- Build your brand.

Chapter 6

USING CONTEMPORARY TECHNOLOGY

One of the major benefits of contemporary technology is that it equips us with tools to enable us to contact, connect, communicate, and collaborate, even when we cannot meet (physically or virtually).

What is the issue?

- There are so many tools available, and you don't know how to use most of the features in the ones you already have.

- You feel as though you are falling behind; everyone appears to be far better at this stuff than you are.

- You can't afford to sign-up for everything, even if each one only costs a little per month.

- If you are going to make an impact in a virtual world, you feel as though you need to be using the latest and greatest.

Why does it matter?

- Using effective and efficient tools can increase your impact and save you time ... but, "Which ones?"

- There is no **best** tool and, even if there was, it may be obsolete tomorrow.

- Those with whom you need to work, and those you need to impact, are making increasing use of contemporary technology.

- To make an impact in a virtual world, you need to be able to speak to that world ... but, you don't have to be the equivalent of Shakespeare in it!

What can you do?

If you are worrying about how you can ever get up-to-speed on the latest technology, then, like many of us, you may be someone who never will. Don't worry. You are far from alone.

The early adopters just get stuck-in and are always ahead of the game – it's what they do. Don't panic! You don't have to be the same.

Frankly, sometimes it is better to wait and see what sticks; there have been thousands of apparently amazing products that are no longer around!

You need to think again about your brand and your target audience. That will tell you who you need to engage actively with, and the types of communication that you will need to use to do that, e.g.,

- Thousands of people or a few selected individuals

- Communicate rarely but with precision and effect, or communicate almost continuously, drip feeding ideas, …

- Sending out specific responses to critical events or spreading the word that you are a guru on certain things

- ….

Actively connect with a selected range of people who represent the type of people you need to influence. Ask them:

- What tools do you use?

- How do you use them?

- Why?

- What measurable benefits have you experienced?

If they are in a similar position to you i.e., trying to achieve impact (rather than being a target), also ask:

- Was your use of them worth the combination of cost and effort to use?

Based on that data, you may wish to consider adding one or two tools to your portfolio, perhaps a:

- Social media site where your targets feature strongly.

- A collaboration site where you can post discussions to build your credibility and perhaps collect research data.

- A file-sharing tool to enable you to create interactions with informed others.

- A polling or survey solution to enable you to poll your target population on their views or perhaps survey others to collect research data.

- A shared whiteboard to enable you to conduct collaborative sessions.

- An interactive webinar tool to enable you to run virtual workshops.

- An artificial intelligence site to challenge your thinking ... no, just joking. They are not here ... YET!

Also, review where you are active. Are the tools you currently use working for you. If not, why not? Is it because of the tools or because of how you use them. Be ruthless! You may need to drop one or more.

As a last recommendation, irrespective of your responses to the above, if you are going to make a positive impact virtually, you do need to invest in:

- A high-quality webcam
- A high-quality unidirectional microphone[6]
- A high-quality speaker
- Suitable lighting
- A professional background for any video shots of you.

Some Additional Thoughts

Here are some further ideas for you to consider:

---

[6] The microphone and speaker may come as a headset. You need to decide whether or not you wish to be seen wearing a headset. If not, then a separate speaker (to ensure that you can hear and understand others) and unidirectional microphone (i.e., it does not pick up peripheral sound) may be more suitable. Note: you can also buy microphones that can operate as unidirectional or omnidirectional.

- Next time you need to work with other people, stop and ask yourself, "Do we need to do this together (i.e., at the same time), or could we make contributions separately?"

There are many tools available now that support very effective asynchronous work, e.g.,

- File sharing. This enables individuals to all access the same file and make changes (which are tracked so that others can see who changed what). Some even provide alerts when changes have been made so that you can re-access the file and view the new changes.

- Social media collaboration sites. These can often be branded, have restricted access, support groups of individuals, etc. and support rolling conversations about a topic until a consensus is reached.

- Polling or survey solutions. These enable the posting of an issue with questions about it. Responses coming back can be shared with the group or merely with the organizer.

- Shared whiteboards. There is a range of tools that support individuals, subject to being provided appropriate access, to visit a whiteboard and edit or post content on it, having viewed prior posts and edits by others.

- Interactive webinars. Many webinar tools now support the interactive engagement of attendees, including the above-mentioned features, as well as break-out groups and screen-shares.

Using Contemporary Technology

Make sure that you keep up to date on (i) which collaboration methods work best to suit your personal impact needs, and (ii) which ones are currently available to you and those you wish to impact.

- Identify those instances when a virtual meeting is the best (efficient and effective) means of collaborating. Typically, this is going to be when (i) you have an issue that requires collaboration, and you want to ensure that everyone gets the same briefing prior to going away and starting work on it, or (ii) you seek to ratify a decision that has largely been made. Take action as appropriate.

Chapter 7

MAKING "LUMPY" VIRTUAL IMPACT

"Lumpy" is used to refer to anything physical such as a letter, a postcard, a copy of an article with a note on it, a flyer, a brochure, a give-away, ….

What is the issue?

- We now live in a world of that communicates in **Connectives**, brief, transient connections between people, processes, and things; across space, time, languages, and cultures.

- It is a largely digital, virtual, and noisy world in which attention spans are short and reducing, and the number of instances of miscommunication is increasing.

- We have dramatically reduced our use of "lumpy" communication.

Why does it matter?

- The rapid expansion in use of social media and email may have driven down the use of "lumpy" connections. However, that rarity is increasing the impact that these lumpy connections now have.

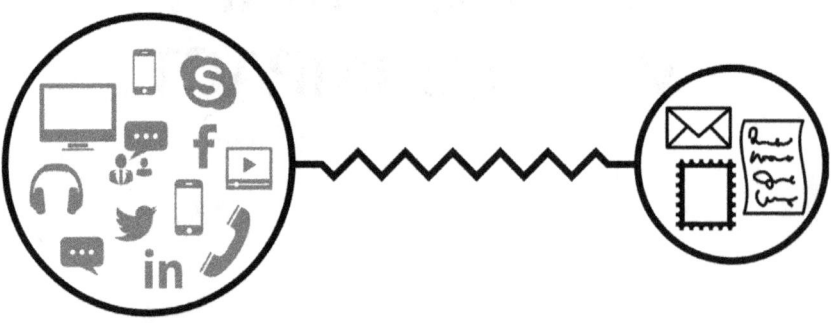

What can you do?

Think about who you need to influence and how. "Lumpy mail" might be a very effective way of doing so. Many will not be receiving much lumpy mail, so you could stand out.

Last year I visited two clients, both of whom I have known for years. I was staggered to find that each of them had, on their desks, boldly displayed, two "lumpy" items that I had sent them previously.

One was an "Executive Survival Kit." It was a small cardboard briefcase with "Executive Survival Kit" printed on the outside. Inside it has a variety of contents including a small pencil, a band-aid, a toothpick, …. It also had a List of Contents, e.g.,

- Pencil ... to enable you to take note of the good in others

- Band-aid ... to remind you not merely to address the symptom but to cure the real cause

- Toothpick ... to remind you not to be too picky; your way may not be the best way

- ....

Even though many have now used this type of concept, it still remained visible with my contact details boldly displayed.

The other was an origami brochure explaining my services to help organizations change their culture through behavior engineering. The brochure was a single sheet of thick paper approximately 8½ inches square but very ingeniously folded into a shape that hid the key contents on the inside ... it was itself a feat of engineering!

Each of those "lumpy" items had my contact details clearly displayed, contained details of what I do, and ... most importantly ... provoked people to ask, "What is that?" and then to play with it.

Think about whether your need to make a virtual impact may be an opportunity to use something "lumpy" e.g.:

- A handwritten letter

- A postcard

- A memorable piece of literature

- A copy of an article (perhaps by you or in support of your views and what you do) with a handwritten note on it

- A credit card for a free coffee

- A tea bag attached to your message

- Your resume

- ….

A colleague of mine had trouble getting materials into the hands of Senior HR Executives. Sending them through the post had failed. Clearly, "gatekeepers" had intervened and thrown them away. Email had not worked; spam filters were seeing to that!

Her solution was simple. She put the materials in a high-quality envelope. She then visited the reception of each target company and explained, "I need these materials to get to your Head of HR." She showed the receptionist that the envelope only contained paperwork, and then sealed it. "Could you please ensure that this gets to the Head of HR, as it is rather important. And, here is something for your trouble. THANK YOU." She then gave the receptionist a high-quality chocolate bar.

The combination of chocolate and reciprocity is very impactful!

EPILOGUE

You now live in a world of that communicates in **Connectives**, brief, transient connections between people, processes, and things; across space, time, languages, and cultures.

It is a largely digital, virtual, and noisy world in which attention spans are short and reducing, and the number of instances of miscommunication is increasing.

Your relationships with others, and thus your potential to impact and influence them, are built from these many **connectives**.

If you are to succeed, you need to manage your Impact Virtually.

APPENDIX 1
PERSONAL BRAND WORKSHEET

The following worksheet can be downloaded as an editable document from: http://clintonwingrove.com/ivfreestuff

> **1. What are you perceived to believe in and value?**
> e.g., Do you put personal gain before others; do you believe in being a team player; do you value relationships; do you insist on ethical business; ...?
>
> **2. What personality traits are you perceived to display?**
> Personality trait theory currently suggests that individual personalities are made up of five broad dispositions[7]:

---

[7] Digman, J.M. (1990). "Personality structure: Emergence of the five-factor model." Annual Review of Psychology. 41

Extraversion:
This is about the extent to which you seem to draw energy from interacting with those around you. Adjectives others would use about you could include: sociable, amiable, excitable, talkative, assertive, emotional.

Agreeableness:
This is about the extent to which you demonstrate empathy and a willingness to connect with others. Adjectives others would use about you could include: kind, affectionate, trusting, compassionate, respectful, cooperative, collaborative.

Conscientiousness:
This is about the extent to which you demonstrate use goal-directed behavior and control any impulsiveness. Adjectives others would use about you could include results-oriented, organized, keen, determined, detail-oriented, dutiful, thoughtful, resilient.

Neuroticism[8]***:*** This is about the extent to which you demonstrate or not calmness and self-control. Positive adjectives others would use about you could include: calm, predictable, stable, self-assured, contented. Negative adjectives others would use about you could include: irritable, moody, stressed, emotional (unstable), anxious, unpredictable.

Openness: This is about the extent to which you demonstrate are open to ideas and experiences. Adjectives others would use about you could include: curious, creative, innovative, open-minded.

---

[8] This is now often replaced with the positive alternative "Emotional Stability."

Personal Brand Worksheet

3. What adjectives apply to you?
There is a list of positive ones available at:
http://clintonwingrove.com/ivfreestuff

4. What are your perceived strengths?
Think about:

- Leadership; your knowledge and skills that enable you to create and bring a vision of the future alive, and secure the resources and commitment to deliver it.

- Management; your knowledge and skills that enable you to make things happen and optimize the use of resources to deliver the vision.

- Business Acumen; your knowledge and skills that enable you to operate in a complex and changing business environment (including in your technical/specialist field).

- Personal Effectiveness; your knowledge and skills that enable you to deliver optimal personal performance, impact, and contributions.

5. What are your perceived limitations?
Think about:

- Leadership; your knowledge and skills that enable you to create and bring a vision of the future alive, and secure the resources and commitment to deliver it.

- Management; your knowledge and skills that enable you to make things happen and optimize the use of resources to deliver the vision.

- Business Acumen; your knowledge and skills that enable you to operate in a complex and changing business environment (including in your technical/specialist field).

- Personal Effectiveness; your knowledge and skills that enable you to deliver optimal personal performance, impact, and contributions.

6. What do people see you as a source of?
Why do they come to; what outputs do you produce; ...?

7. When do people feel you should be avoided?
What's known to frustrate you; when, if ever, do you have bad moods; ...?

8. If you were a product, what would 'the market' (other people) use as your tag-line?
e.g., He's the Excel guru; She's the one who will smash the glass ceiling; If you want very direct feedback, he's the one you'll get it from; She'll step on anyone to get what she wants; Tell them what you know and the world will know in seconds; ...

APPENDIX 2
DISRESPECTFUL BEHAVIORS

Put a tick (✓) in the left box if you ever experience the behavior. Think about how it made you feel. These may adversely affect your ability to create a positive impact if you display them to others.

	1. Not listening to or considering others' opinions and perspectives
	2. Chronically complaining and being negative
	3. Making discriminatory comments
	4. Inappropriately CC'ing or BCC'ing others on emails
	5. Speaking negatively about others behind their backs
	6. Ignoring, excluding, and ostracizing others
	7. Speaking loudly or discussing personal matters in a public area

	8. Lying or giving misleading information
	9. Saying one thing and doing another - hypocritical
	10. Refusing to accept responsibility for their mistakes
	11. Using vulgar language or inappropriate behavior; making inappropriate "jokes" or sarcastic remarks
	12. Not giving full attention to others when they are speaking, e.g., checking email, SMS
	13. Interrupting others while they are speaking
	14. Jumping to conclusions and being presumptuous
	15. Failing to fulfill on job responsibilities or commitments
	16. Making excessive use of social media or personal phone calls
	17. Bragging about their own accomplishments
	18. Raising their voice unnecessarily
	19. Rambling or dominating conversations
	20. Over-stepping boundaries – personal and/or professional
	21. Passing the buck; dumping work or blaming their shortcomings on others
	22. Taking credit for others' accomplishments
	23. Arriving late to meetings or calls, and/or being unprepared
	24. Not following-through or getting back to people in a timely manner
	25. Being publicly critical of others' and their ideas

DISRESPECTFUL BEHAVIORS

The above list is kindly provided by Dr. Paul Marciano, author of "Carrots & Sticks Don't Work," McGaw-Hill, and co-author with Clinton Wingrove of "SuperTeams: using the principles of RESPECT to unleash explosive business performance," McGaw-Hill.

This checklist is available to download at:
http://clintonwingrove.com/ivfreestuff

IMPACT VIRTUALLY PRODUCTS & SERVICES

Impact Virtually is a range of products and services which equip individuals to achieve greater influence in what is an increasingly noisy, virtual, and largely digital world.

For further information and products and services in the Impact Virtually range, visit:

http://clintonwingrove.com/IV

For other products and services, visit:

http://clintonwingrove.com/home

For information on how Clinton Wingrove and his team can partner with your organization to unleash potential and transform performance, visit:

http://clintonhr.com/home

This booklet is part of a wider range of products and services to equip individuals, teams, and organizations to "**Unleash their potential and transform their performance**."

www.ingramcontent.com/pod-product-compliance
Lightning Source LLC
Chambersburg PA
CBHW071724020426
42333CB00017B/2386